1

TABLE OF CONTENTS

ABBREVIATIONS AND ACRONYMS

ACTESA	Alliance for Commodity Trade in Eastern and Southern Africa
AfDB	African Development Bank
AFFM	African Fertilizer Financing Mechanism
AGRHYMET	Centre Régional de Formation et d'Application en Agro météorologie et Hydrologie Opérationnelle
AGRA	Alliance for a Green Revolution in Africa
AOPP	Association des Organisations Professionnelles Paysannes
ATP	Agribusiness and Trade Promotion project
BFS	Bureau of Food Security
CILSS	Permanent Interstate Committee for Drought Control in the Sahel
CAADP	Comprehensive African Agriculture Development Program
CBC	Burkina Shippers' Council
CGIAR	Consultative Group on International Agricultural Research
CORAF	West and Central Africa Council for Agricultural Research and Development
E-ATP	Expanded Agribusiness and Trade Promotion project
ECOWAS	Economic Community of West African States
ECOWAP	Economic Community of West African States Agriculture Policy
ETLS	ECOWAS Trade Liberalization Scheme
FAO	Food and Agriculture Organization
FTF	Feed the Future
GCC	Global Climate Change
GIS	Geographical Information Systems
ha	hectares
HKI	Helen Keller Institute
IARC	International Agricultural Research Center
ICRISAT	International Crops Research Institute for the Semi-Arid
ILO	International Labor Organization
IR	Intermediate Result
ISAP	Improved Sustainable Agricultural Productivity
IFDC	International Center for Soil Fertility and Agricultural Development
IFPRI	International Food Policy Research Institute
IWMI	International Water Management Institute
kg	kilograms
MCC	Millennium Challenge Corporation
MDG	Millennium Development Goal
M&E	Monitoring and Evaluation
MIS	Market Information System
MT	Metric Ton
MUS	Multiple-use Services
NARS	National Agricultural Research Systems
NEPAD	New Partnership for Africa's Development
NGO	Non-governmental Organization
NPC	Non-Presence Country
OFDA	Office of Foreign Disaster Assistance
RAO	Regional Agriculture
ROECCR	Regional Office on Environment and Climate Change Response
RTAAF	Regional Technical Agency for Agriculture and Food
RTIO	Regional Trade and Investment Office (USAID/WA)

ROPPA	Regional Network of Peasant and Agricultural Producer Organizations
RECAO	Réseau des Chambres d'Agriculture de l'Ouest
ROESAO	Réseau des Opérateurs Economiques du Secteur Agroalimentaire de L'Afrique de L'Ouest
ReSAKSS	Regional Strategic Analysis and Knowledge Support System
SPS	Sanitary and Phyto-Sanitary
Sub-IR	Sub-Intermediate Result
UEMOA	West Africa Economic and Monetary Union
USADF	United States African Development Fund
USDA	United States Department of Agriculture
USGS	United States Geological Survey
USG	United States Government
WASA	West African Seed Alliance
WA	West Africa
WA-WASH	West African Water and Sanitation for Health Project

I. CHALLENGES AND OPPORTUNITIES

West Africa is one of the poorest regions in the world. A full fifty-four percent of West Africans live below the poverty line, and if present trends continue, there will be more poor people in West Africa in 2015 than in 1990.[1] At present, no West African state, except Ghana, is on trend to meet the first Millennium Development Goal (MDG) of halving poverty and malnutrition by 2015. Approximately 37 percent of children five years or younger in West Africa are under height for their age; 28 percent are underweight; and 10 percent of children are affected by acute malnutrition. Nutritional deficits are more common in women and children, and, geographically, in the Sahel states and the drier northern areas of coastal countries.

USAID is committed through the Feed the Future (FTF) Initiative to regain momentum in addressing persistent poverty and hunger. USAID/West Africa's overarching FTF goal is to assist countries in West Africa in achieving MDG 1, Eradicating Hunger and Extreme Poverty.

To achieve MDG 1, West Africa would need to annually reduce poverty by 5.2 percent. If the region's agriculture was to grow at 6.8 percent annually, West Africa as a whole would be able to halve poverty by 2015. Such rapid growth will require a substantial increase in public and private investments to transform production for West Africa's food markets and widen access.

This document represents the U.S. Government's (USG) Multi-year Strategy under FTF. It reflects a highly integrated approach spanning the areas of Agriculture, Environment, Health and Trade and Investment, which accounts for its multi-faceted nature. USAID/West Africa (WA) will avail itself of the staff, expertise, and financial resources of these four offices to design and implement an interdisciplinary program that attacks poverty and food insecurity from a variety of angles.

1.1 CHALLENGES

There are several root causes of poverty and food insecurity in West Africa. Roughly 70 percent of the region's population relies on agriculture for their livelihood.[2] Smallholder farming in West Africa is characterized by rain-fed production, low fertilizer use, poor quality seeds, inadequate water management, and low soil fertility. As a result, per-hectare yields in West Africa are some of the lowest in the world. In short, the Green Revolution has yet to take hold.

The region's stagnation in agricultural productivity is integrally linked to systemic weaknesses in policies, markets, and trade. Although the Economic Community of West Africa States (ECOWAS) Trade Liberalization Scheme (ETLS) was adopted in 1990 – permitting free trade of goods across borders, none of the eight[3] ECOWAS countries examined in depth[4] fully adhere to ETLS protocols. The eight countries review averaged just under sixty percent implementation of the agreement on free movement of goods. The results is that West African markets are fragmented, weakening the incentives to invest in more productive agricultural technologies and contributing to a lack of availability of staple foods and the volatility of their prices. Moreover, transportation in the region is the most expensive in the world (on a per kilometer basis), which significantly increases the cost of agriculture inputs.

---

[1] Johnson Michael. et al; Regional Strategic Alternatives for Agriculture-led Growth and Poverty Reduction in West Africa, ReSAKSS Working Paper No. 22; November 2008, page 23.
[2] Ibid, page 24
[3] Benin, Burkina, Côte d'Ivoire, Ghana, Niger, Nigeria, Mali, and Togo
[4] Gap Analysis: ECOWAS Free Trade Area. USAID/West Africa Trade Hub. December 2009.

Demographic trends in West Africa pose additional challenges to food security. Food production has not kept pace with its growing population. As a result, West Africa relies increasingly on food imports at international prices to feed itself. The region suffered as global prices for food rose in 2007 and 2008. Demographers anticipate that West Africa's population will continue to grow rapidly, rising from 290 million to reach 430 million by 2025.[5] Population growth will be accompanied by high levels of urbanization. At present rates, 60 percent of the population will be urban dwellers by 2020.

1.2   OPPORTUNITIES AND USAID/WEST AFRICA'S COMPARATIVE ADVANTAGE

While bilateral programs can address national level constraints to food security such as strengthening a national agriculture extension service to improve agricultural productivity, only a regional program can address issues that cut across national borders. As a regional program, USAID/WA is well situated to address constraints such as supporting regional policy reform and implementation, building the capacity of regional institutions, supporting regional investments in hard and soft infrastructure, and promoting deeper regional integration. All these interventions can increase trade and positively impact the livelihoods and food security of poor people. Regional programs and integration with bilateral efforts can unleash powerful multipliers leading to faster growth and reduced poverty and hunger.

Using its regional position, USAID/WA will engage in programs to increase agriculture productivity, provide market opportunities to farmers and traders, and increase food security. Trade is a powerful engine of growth and a means to ensuring broad availability of food, particularly for smaller countries. Often the barriers to trade are greatest at local and regional borders. The Mission's regionally focused projects and programs have the potential to encourage freer flow of transport and trade and establish common standards for food safety and quality. Its efforts to support ECOWAS in regional integration can also facilitate the flow of information, knowledge, and improved technologies across national borders.

> **A Business Model: USAID/West Africa And Bilateral Coordination**
>
> To better coordinate and capitalize on mutual efforts to promote food security in the region, USAID/WA and bilateral mission representatives formed an advisory board that consults regularly on strategic and implementation issues. The strategic integration of bilateral and regional programs can produce transformational results since missions tackle constraints from different perspectives and build on each other's successes.
>
> In developing its FTF strategy, USAID/WA has taken advantage of the board to discuss planned components -- building consensus and integrating important bilateral perspectives. As the Mission moves forward to implement the strategy – especially with the design of new activities – the advisory board will continue to play a prominent role.

As a regional Mission, USAID/WA can effectively engage in activities such as harmonization of regional trade and inputs policies; development and dissemination of agricultural technology; and capacity building of regional public, private, and civil society organizations. It can also tackle cross-border operational issues such as trade rules, sanitary and phyto-sanitary (SPS) regulations as well as other wide-spread problems such as global climate change, famine and conflict. Moreover, USAID/WA's regional mandate increases the impact of agricultural research by advancing the work of West and Central African Council for Agricultural Research and Development (CORAF) and Permanent Inter-State Committee for Drought Control in the Sahel (CILSS). CORAF and CILSS add value by coordinating a common research agenda among West Africa's national research centers to continuously develop disease and drought resistant varieties for common agro-ecological zones.

---

[5] Ibid, page 18

Lastly, as a regional mission, USAID/WA is best placed to strengthen core regional organizations such as ECOWAS and the West African Economic and Monetary Union (UEMOA), which play a key role in providing alternatives to nationally focused trade and agricultural policies. ECOWAS provides the forum for engaging national governments to harmonize policies for plant and animal health requirements, fertilizer and seed standards, border measures, and transport regulation – all crucial to the integration of West Africa's agricultural markets. Moreover, the Mission's mandate enables regional activities to develop a more competitive trade and transport network and to enhance the flow of market linkages and information across national borders.

1.3   CROSS CUTTING ISSUES

USAID/WA has identified a number of cross cutting issues important to achieving its FTF objectives.

1.3.1   Nutrition

USAID/WA's regional focus limits the possibilities for direct, country specific interventions in nutrition. However, the Mission is ideally positioned to support regional actors involved in nutrition monitoring and research as well as provide support in addressing cross-border nutritional issues, such as food safety. Additionally, progress towards increasing volume while reducing cost of regional trade in staple and other nutritionally important foods will lead to cheaper foods, higher incomes, and overall economic growth that will benefit the poor nutritionally.

USAID/WA will achieve maximum impact with the $700,000 in nutrition funds received yearly by continuing the partnership with Helen Keller International (HKI) to promote vitamin A fortification of cooking oil in select countries in the region. Working with HKI, the Mission engages West African governments and institutions to accelerate mandatory vitamin A fortification, providing assistance to develop and pass laws to harmonize fortification policies and standards. USAID/WA also leverages other donor funds – aiming to reach 70 percent of the population with fortified foods to address serious vitamin and mineral deficiencies, especially prominent among women and children. The ultimate objectives of this activity are to ensure that Vitamin A fortification of cooking oil and wheat flour is mandatory in all ECOWAS countries and that there is widespread awareness of and demand for such products in the region.

Also on the nutrition front, the work described below on improving the efficiency of regional market transactions will include capacity building for cereal growers on control of mycotoxins (especially aflatoxin), which enable them to access new markets for their products, including multinational companies making baby food. In addition to expanding trade, such activities also have clear benefits with respect to nutrition and public health.

1.3.2 Gender

Evidence exists to show that gender disparities in access to and control over different types of assets have negative impacts on growth in the agriculture sector.[6] In West Africa, gender disparities are severe and are likely to continue to inhibit economic growth.

USAID/WA's regional focus presents broad opportunities to support programs to reform regional policies inhibiting women's access to business and trading opportunities and to work closely with regional organizations such as ECOWAS to assist with linking existing gender policies with program implementation. The Mission will also develop and use gender-equitable approaches in its programs to improve agricultural production, regional trade, and capacity building for agricultural sector actors. Programs will be designed and implemented to factor in the impacts on the different roles and responsibilities of both women and men within a given activity. Program design and development will ensure the distinctive needs of women are met in such areas as: fostering equitable participation and resource allocation enterprises; encouraging equitable participation of women in all levels of decision-making; promoting gender analysis by policy analysts and makers; and increasing understanding of the performance of USAID investments in reducing gender inequities in agriculture, trade, and capacity building programs.

1.3.3 Climate Change

Although the effects of climate change and variability on agricultural production are not yet fully understood, the region's vulnerabilities are reasonably clear. West Africa is undergoing changes in temperature and rainfall, with some areas experiencing reoccurring drought. River flows and the recharging of aquifers are declining (not all due to changes in climate); extreme events are more frequent; and coastal areas are experiencing rises in sea level and increased soil erosion. The West African National Adaptation Program of Action identified the priority vulnerable areas requiring attention as: water resources, agriculture and livestock, coastal zones, forestry, and the overall need for capacity-building and increased public awareness.

According to the Food and Agriculture Organization (FAO), one way to build adaptive capacity and climate resilient production systems is through improved soil and water management techniques that can increase soil organic matter, nutrients, and moisture – reducing the overall crop vulnerability. Climate-smart agriculture is a key element in Mission programs to improve sustainable agricultural productivity.

---

[6] Barrett Nichols, K., C Manfre and D. Rubin, *Promoting Gender Equitable Opportunities: Why it Matters for Agricultural Value Chains.* Washington, D.C. USAID 2009. N. Birdsall, et. al.; "Inequality and Growth Revisited: Lessons from East Asia," *World Bank Economic Review* 9, 1995. Deininger, K. and L Squire, "New Ways of Looking at Old Issues: Inequality and Growth." *Journal of Development Economics* 57, 1998. Sabates-Wheeler, R.:, *Asset Inequality and Agricultural Growth: How Are Patterns of Asset Inequality Established and Reproduced;* Brighton, UK; IDS, 2004.

2. STRATEGIC OVERVIEW: WEST AFRICA REGIONAL FEED THE FUTURE RESULTS FRAMEWORK

2.1 THE RESULTS FRAMEWORK

The USG has employed a rigorous analytic approach to developing its Feed the Future strategy and results framework (Figure 1). The initial conceptualization of the basic framework for the FTF strategy was informed by analyses focusing on three overarching questions:

1. What are the critical challenges and issues directly impacting food security that are regional in nature (versus nationally-based) and can best be addressed by a regional approach?

2. Is there evidence that addressing these constraints will have substantial impact?

3. Where is the strongest alignment of USAID/WA's priorities and comparative advantage – technical expertise and field experience – with those issues best addressed through regional actions?

The Mission then both narrowed the strategic focus of its FTF strategy and built a highly integrated strategy by applying four "strategic filters." These filters include:

1. Target a small number of agricultural commodities: Focus the FTF strategic approach and programming on those commodities that will have a strong and direct impact on regional food security and will also substantially benefit from USAID interventions and expertise.

2. Address limited segments of value chains: Emphasize the transactional components of value chains, recognizing that the most effective point of impact for regional interventions focuses on elements necessary for efficient market transactions. (Bilateral missions and partners are better positioned to address production and processing segments of value chains.)

3. Maximize the impact of USAID bilateral missions: Understanding that progress across West Africa is dependent on simultaneously addressing related opportunities and constraints at both a regional and national scale as well as promote coordinated efforts to address policy constraints and agricultural productivity. This filter also recognizes the Mission's dual role: to plan and manage regional programs and to support and collaborate with bilateral missions.

4. Use a "model to scale" approach: Recognize that it will be appropriate and useful at times to identify and target work towards those specific agro-ecologies or commodities that offer the highest likelihood of success while also providing important learning for eventually expanding efforts to other sub-regions and commodities.

Based on these strategic filters and core considerations, the USG developed a FTF strategy that pursues *Increased Food Security in West Africa* by focusing both on *Improved Sustainable Agricultural Productivity (Intermediate Result 1)* and *Increased Regional Trade in Key Agricultural Commodities (Intermediate Result 2)*. This overarching strategic approach – or development hypothesis – recognizes the necessity to address relevant policy and increased productivity as a means to increase the volume of food staples produced across the region as well as more effectively move commodities from areas of production (surplus) to areas of consumption (deficit). Simply put, the core of the Mission's strategy to improve regional food security aims to lower costs and expand markets in ways that make agricultural technologies good investments for smallholder farmers. More efficient regional production of food traded across borders will reduce price volatility and lower prices, benefiting consumers and reducing West Africa's dependence on imported food.

Recognizing the weaknesses in key organizations and institutions with large roles to play in developing regional agriculture and trade, USAID/WA has included a supporting/capacity building Intermediate Result. Underpinning the core strategy is *Intermediate Result 3, Increased Capacity of Regional Agricultural Sector Actors*. Interventions aimed at this result will support both public and private sector institutions and associations.

Intermediate Result 1 encompasses two dimensions of agricultural productivity. The first sub-result, *Increased Use of Climate-Smart Agricultural Practices*, recognizes that a large portion of the farming population of West Africa – mostly smallholders – live and farm in regions with marginal growing conditions. In order to facilitate long term productivity gains, while enhancing the condition of the land and natural resource base, the Mission aims to expand the use of climate-smart agriculture practices in selected regions in the Sahel. The second sub-result, *Increased Availability of Improved Agricultural Inputs*, addresses the potential to substantially increase yields and overall production of commodities in areas where climatic conditions are favorable to relatively intensive agriculture – areas with good soils and substantial rainfall and/or the potential to use irrigation. This sub-result aims to increase the use of improved inputs – predominantly high yielding varieties of seeds and fertilizer. Combined, these sub-IRs target farms across a range of sizes and production systems.

To increase the use of climate-smart agriculture practices, the USG strategy calls for active collaboration with selected bilateral missions, including USAID/Ghana and USAID/Mali. USAID/WA will focus on the development and dissemination of knowledge on the use of climate-smart agriculture practices (e.g., what combination of practices is most productive and practical, given specific farm conditions and characteristics) and on better concentrating climate-smart agriculture interventions in areas that have the potential to benefit most from the technology. Increased use of climate-smart agriculture practices will, however, also require a high level of collaboration and bilateral involvement to drive widespread adoption at the farm level across the region. Regional organizations (CORAF and CILSS) and bilateral missions will work with national organizations to help farmers learn about climate-smart agriculture and to ensure the necessary inputs are available to drive widespread adoption.

The agricultural inputs component of the productivity Intermediate Result focuses on increasing the availability of seeds of high yielding varieties and fertilizer for rice and maize and distribution of these inputs; a result supported, in turn, by promoting policy reform and private sector development. Increased availability of inputs is also dependent on outcomes related to improved market and transport efficiencies pursued through the Mission's trade program. In fact, this portion of the FTF strategy reflects the most substantial integration of multiple projects, that is, improved efficiencies in market transactions and reduced transport costs not only support increased regional trade in key agricultural commodities, but also increased regional availability of seeds and fertilizer.

Moving from agricultural productivity (IR 1) to regional trade in agricultural commodities (IR 2), the USG's FTF strategy identifies three results that will drive increased levels of trade. We expect to achieve the first of these results, *Improved Competitiveness of the Transport and Logistics Sector*, by addressing existing constraints to efficient market operations, including a lack of market information; an insufficient range and availability of financial services; and poor buyer-seller networking and communication. The second result supporting IR 2, *Reduced Legal and Regulatory Barriers to Trade*, focuses on encouraging investment and efficiency in transportation of food staples and inputs, including addressing road governance (bribes) and other issues along key corridors. Finally, the third sub-result, *Improved Efficiency of Regional Market Transactions*, aims to address overarching regional constraints

Figure I. West Africa Feed the Future Results Framework

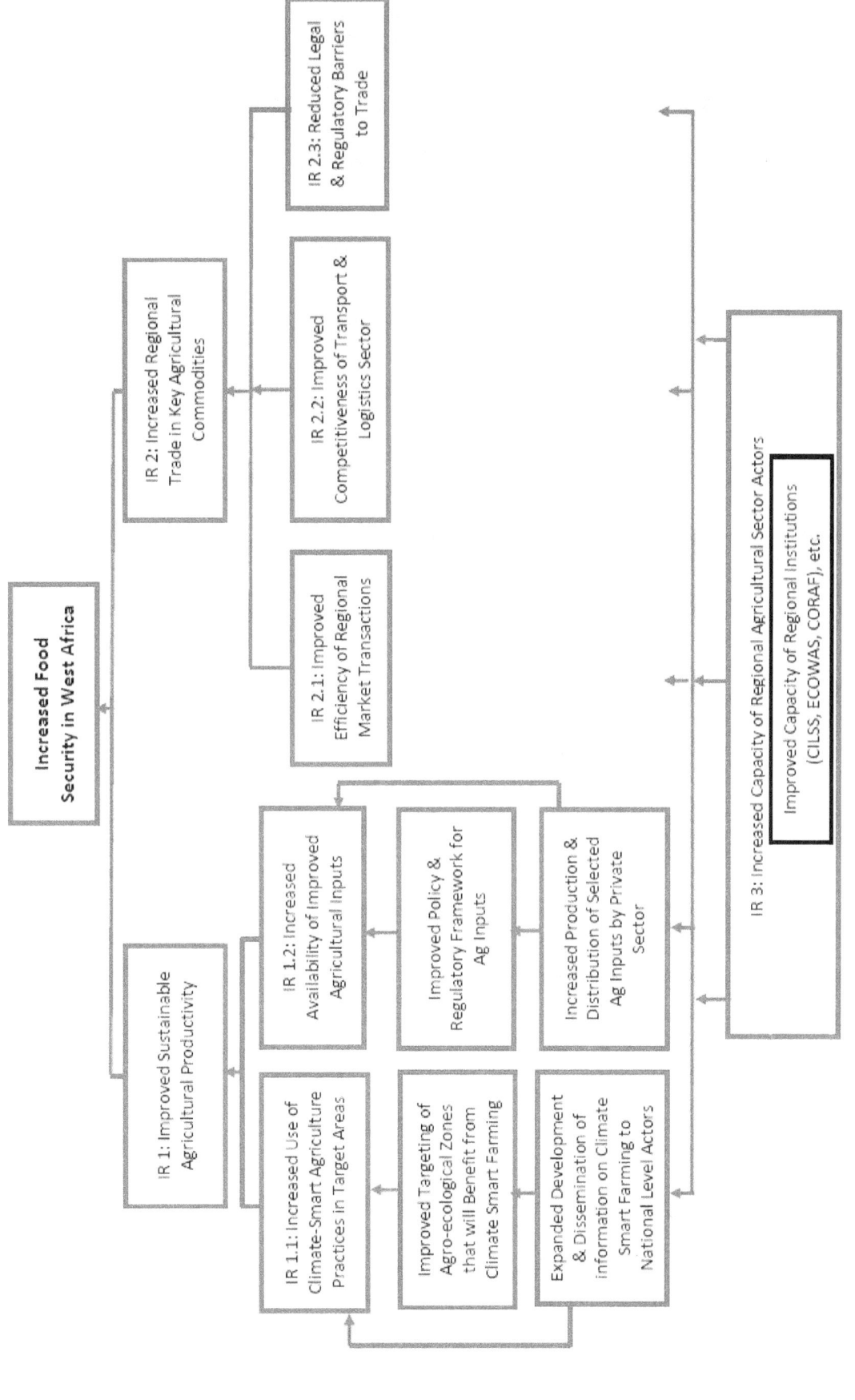

11

through the harmonization of regional policies relevant to agricultural inputs and products, and country-to-country policies and regulations.

In summary, by achieving substantial improvements in the efficiency of market transactions, by markedly reducing transport and logistics costs related to the movement of agricultural commodities, and by reducing regulatory constraints at both the broad regional level and the country-to-country level, the Mission expects notable increases in the level of regional trade in key agricultural commodities critically important to food security, such as maize. Taken together with increasing agricultural productivity of important food security crops, both in zones with high production potential and in more fragile and marginal production zones, the Mission expects to have an important impact on food security in the region. Importantly, the Mission's FTF strategy purposely targets the interaction between trade and productivity, i.e., that increased regional trade in agricultural products will help drive increased productivity, just as increased productivity will generate expanded trade.

2.2   STRATEGIC CHOICES

It is important to stress that, while the West Africa region encompasses the 15 ECOWAS member states with a combined surface area of 5.1 million square kilometers and population of 300 million inhabitants, the Mission will be highly selective with respect to the commodities on which to focus the productivity and value chain-related work as well as in the selection of geographical focus.

Strategic Choice – Narrowing the Focus

The Mission's effort to focus its strategy is illustrated by its decision to emphasize maize and rice under agricultural inputs. Strategic considerations informing this decision, included:

- Maize and rice breeder seed exists, allowing for relatively rapid ramp-up of certified seed production for distribution and sale.

- Maize and rice have a high impact on food security. Rice is the number one staple crop consumed in West Africa.

- Maize is a highly commercialized commodity and is effectively addressed by both the agricultural productivity and regional trade components of the FTF strategy, thus facilitating cross-project management and synergies allowing for improved progress towards FTF results.

- Focusing on a narrow set of commodities allows for use of a "model to scale" approach, through which a structural model for input development and distribution or cross-border commodity trade can be developed.

Value Chains

USAID/WA has selected as its highest priority value chains the major **cereals** (i.e., maize, millet, rice, and sorghum) and **livestock**. These value chains were selected based on their: 1) importance to intra-regional trade; 2) high potential for value addition; 3) production by large numbers of smallholders; and 4) synergies with other supported value chains (e.g., maize is used as livestock feed).

Maize, millet, and sorghum together account for about a third of all calories consumed by West Africans. Maize is particularly critical to food security for both human and animal consumption. The relatively large level of intra-regional trade is primarily the result of differences in the timing and number of growing seasons in neighboring countries, a fact that results in reversals in net trade flows over the course of the year. In 2007, 19 percent of the maize imported by ECOWAS countries came from within the region (as compared with rice where nearly all was imported from outside). Additionally, the maize value chain is important to other key value chains in the region. For example, yellow maize – most of which is currently imported from outside the region – is a main ingredient in poultry feed, and in processing products from flour to baby food. Among bilateral USAID missions, Ghana and Senegal have also selected maize as one of their value chains, opening considerable possibilities for collaboration.

Millet and sorghum are the major components of the diet of many of the region's poorest rural people, especially in the Sahel. Problems in the supply of these coarse grains are closely linked to food crises such as that in Niger in 2005. Although often viewed as a "poor man's food," there is growing interest in trade in processed foods produced with millet and sorghum.[7] Among bilateral USAID missions in West Africa, Mali and Senegal have selected millet and sorghum as one of their respective value chains.

Rice is the most important cereal in the region from a consumption point of view (accounting for 12-13 percent of caloric intake) and its consumption has been growing rapidly.[8] Rice is a priority value chain for all four potential FTF focus countries in West Africa (Ghana, Liberia, Mali, and Senegal). As recognized in the ECOWAP Investment Plan, importing rice from outside the region is an enormous drain on the foreign exchange reserves of all these countries. Ghana, for example, is able to meet only 30 percent of its rice consumption from domestic production, leaving it with an annual rice import bill on the order of $500 million.[9]

Livestock is the largest value item in regional agricultural trade, with annual trade flows in ruminants of $300 million.[10] Some 250 percent growth in demand for livestock products is anticipated for the Sahel and West Africa region by 2025 due to growing urban populations.[11] Meat – and to lesser extent dairy products – is an important source of dietary protein. Trade in animals is generally unidirectional, from the Sahel to the coast. Livestock is the most valuable asset owned by many rural households, so losses of value in transport can have severe consequences. USAID/WA's focus on livestock is further justified by the importance of pastoralists and the environmental aspects of livestock rearing in the Sahel.[12] The livestock value chain is inherently regional, as large numbers of animals move across national boundaries. USAID/Liberia and USAID/Mali have also selected livestock as one of their value chains.

In order to further refine its selection of interventions, USAID/WA will support analytical work that models the effects of specific interventions of a regional nature that will benefit particular value chains and geographical locations. An important aspect of the Mission's program under FTF will be engaging International Food Policy Research Institute (IFPRI) in efforts to model the impacts on economic growth, poverty reduction, and improved nutritional outcomes of highly specific interventions.

---

[7] According to a recent study, "Across the region, value added food products derived from millet/sorghum have the potential to compete with rice and other food preparations for a greater share of household consumption spending. Anecdotal evidence suggests that urban demand across the region currently outstrips production." See "Millet Sorghum: Promoting Regional Food Security Through Trade: Prospects for Value Chain Development," prepared by Abt Associates for USAID/WA, May 2010, p. 9.

8 "Global Food Security Response: West Africa Rice Value Chain Analysis, microReport #161, Study prepared for USAID, October 2009, p. 8.

9 "Ghana's rice imports bill hits $500m" Ghana Business News, January 24, 2009 (http://www.ghanabusinessnews.com/2009/01/24/ghana%E2%80%99s-rice-imports-bill-hits-500m).

[10] By way of comparison, in FY 2010 trade in live ruminants at 13 markets in six countries, as measured by USAID/WA's current agricultural trade facilitation project, amounted to $293 million, as compared to $15 million in maize trade at 18 markets in three countries. Combined trade in millet and sorghum similarly measured came to $26 million in FY 2010.

[11] "Modern and Mobile: The Future of Livestock Production in Africa's Drylands," International Institute for Environment and Development, 2010, p. 23.

[12] Ibid.

Agricultural Inputs

The agricultural inputs component focuses on increasing the availability of high-yield seed varieties and fertilizer for selected food staple crops (maize and rice) and distribution of these inputs; a result supported by building the management and marketing capabilities of a small number of firms with the highest potential for growth for operating regionally. **Maize** and **rice** are the crops for which breeder seed exists, allowing for relatively rapid ramp-up of certified seed production for distribution and sale. As discussed above, maize has a high impact on food security. Rice as well is crucial to food security in West Africa. Rice alone accounts for 12 percent of calories consumed in West Africa, more than any other staple food.

Geographical Foci

Geographically-specific work on trade and transport will be implemented along corridors (and associated border posts) strategically important to regional agricultural trade. According to USAID/WA commissioned research and an iso-price mapping exercise, the steepest price gradients between major producing areas and major population centers appear on the corridors running from Dakar to Niamey, Ouagadougou to coastal Ghana, and Kaduna to Niamey. Mapping of chronically deficit and typically surplus zones for cereals and livestock tells a similar story. These corridors are important for the transport of the commodities on which activities under the strategy will focus (cereals and livestock). Reducing bottlenecks along those corridors and at border points are a high priority from the perspective of improving regional trade flows.

In addition, the borders along the Lagos-Abidjan corridor are also high priority, given the density of coastal populations and the importance of this corridor for conveying cereals from eastern production basins to western markets. About 90 percent of transit traffic in West Africa passes along this corridor, and iso-price mapping revealed persistently high prices in all of these markets. Improving the flow of trade between them would allow for greater competition and smoothing of prices between eastern and western basins.

2.3   CORE INVESTMENT AREAS

The USG has developed a strategy that pursues Increased Food Security in West Africa focusing both on Improved Sustainable Agricultural Productivity (IR 1) and Increased Regional Trade in Key Agricultural Commodities (IR 2). The third area of effort -- Increasing the Capacity of Regional Agricultural Sector Actors (IR3) underpins the strategy through building capacities of public and private entities with mandates in development of agriculture, trade and food security.

Improved Sustainable Agricultural Productivity (Intermediate Result 1**)**

To improve agricultural productivity, the strategy aims at two core investment areas: Increased Use of Climate-smart Agriculture Practices in Target Areas (Core Investment Area 1), and Increased Use of Improved Agricultural Inputs through Increasing Availability, Production and Distribution and Private Sector Marketing (Core Investment Area 2).

Because of the strong link between improved soil and water management and the effective use of inputs, there will be close collaboration between Core Investment Areas 1 and 2. Climate smart agriculture involves identifying and growing crops/plants adapted to present and future climatic changes, whereas agricultural inputs are the raw materials needed by the crops/plants that are grown in the various climatic regimes in West Africa. Because of this relationship, there will be close collaboration between the two programs especially with regard to soil and water management practices under the various regimes. There are clear linkages in terms of crop type, crop variety, and appropriateness of fertilizer with regards to its efficient use by crop and under given soil and moisture regimes.

2.3.1 Core Investment Area 1: Increased Use of Climate-Smart Agriculture Practices

USAID's Regional Offices of Agriculture and of Environment and Climate Change Response will join forces in supporting this core investment area. Feed The Future and Climate Adaptation resources will flow through regional mechanisms focusing on four countries and will support regional institutions, such as CORAF and CILSS. In addition, a new innovative Climate Change activity that seeks to improve regional dissemination and use of climate information in decision-making will complement investments in "climate-smart" agriculture[13] in key agro-ecological zones.

Constraints

Agricultural productivity of many smallholder West African farmers is challenged by poor soil fertility and regular shortages of soil moisture. It is highly likely that shortages in soil moisture will become greater and more variable due to climate change. Climate change will put increasing pressure on West African agricultural systems and water resources already affected by recurring drought. Field research in West Africa has shown that on many soils of the Sahel, the majority of plant nutrients from fertilizer applications are lost to run-off and leaching before being taken up by plants. As a result, the potential impact of improved seeds and fertilizers is limited. Recent studies have shown that one reason for the low adoption of fertilizer may be due to low fertilizer-use efficiency caused by lack of soil organic matter.[14] Soil fertility and moisture constraints can be addressed by a broader application of technologies that increase soil organic matter and rainwater infiltration. Although these practices have shown great success in West Africa – particularly in fragile agro-ecological zones, which span across West Africa – they have not seen wide-spread adoption in agricultural systems across the region.

Re-Greening of the Sahel

During the 1970s and 1980s, West Africa, particularly the arid and semi-arid lands of the Sahel, experienced devastating droughts. These extremes of climatic variability impacted negatively on human livelihoods, agricultural production systems, and the ecological factors that underpin both. In some West African states, particularly Niger, smallholders and government took action to address this situation in the form of farmer-managed natural regeneration of woody species. One result is that more than 4.8 million hectares in Niger are greener today than 20 years ago.

This greening has improved soil and water conservation and increased productivity of annual crops in densely populated and agriculturally over-exploited areas. It is estimated that this transformation in the farming system has resulted in an average of at least 500,000 additional tons of food produced per year in Niger. This experience is considered one of the compelling success stories in the sustainable management of agricultural lands, and suggests that similar positive transformations in farming livelihoods and environmental rehabilitation are possible across the Sahel and even into the more temperate agro-ecological zones of West Africa.

---

[13] Climate-smart agriculture is defined as agriculture that sustainably increases productivity, resilience (adaptation), reduces/removes greenhouse gases (mitigation), and enhances achievement of national food security and development goals (see FAO, *Climate-smart Agriculture: Policies, Practices and Financing for Food Security, Adaptation and Mitigation*, November 2010).

[14] Marenya, P.P. and C.B. Barrett 2009a; *Soil Quality and Fertilizer Use Rates Among Smallholder Farmers in Western Kenya;* American Journal of Agricultural Economics, 40: 561-572.

Marenya, P.P. and C.B. Barrett 2009b; *State-Conditional Fertilizer Yield Response on Western Kenyan Farms;* American Journal of Agricultural Economics, 91(4): 991-1006.

Climate-Smart Production Systems

For agricultural investments to be sustained there is a need to build and maintain "climate-smart production systems"[15]. According to the FAO, key ways in which climate resilience and adaptive capacity can be enhanced are by: improving soil fertility, soil moisture- holding capacity and soil stability; promoting efficient water harvesting; and expanding practices of sustainable land use. These are also critical actions for improving agricultural productivity because they enhance the effectiveness of improved seeds and fertilizers. Other critical investments that farmers have made to enhance climate resiliency are in agro-forestry and in farmer-managed natural regeneration of Sahelian woodlands. These practices diversify smallholder farming systems and help "buffer" them against the impact of climatic variability.

There is a growing body of research that confirms the links between proper soil and water management, increased productivity, and climate resiliency. For example, soil management techniques that combine the use of inorganic fertilizer with compost or manure have generated an average of 50 percent increase in fertilizer use efficiency.[16] Several studies have also shown that rainfall infiltration can be significantly increased through simple soil conservation measures such as "Zai" pits[17], stone bunds, and through conservation agriculture. Comprehensive African Agriculture Development Program (CAADP), recognizing that sustainable soil and water management is vital for increased agricultural productivity, has provided a supportive structure under its Pillar 1, "Sustainable Land and Water Management."

Strategic Context

As a regional Mission, USAID/WA is well-poised to support and enhance the long-term goals of CAADP Pillar 1 - "restoring, sustaining and enhancing the productive and protective functions of Africa's land and water resources by combating the interrelated problems of land degradation, food insecurity and rural poverty"- while also addressing critical climate change concerns.

Specifically, the Mission will support Outcome 2.2 of the ECOWAP Investment Plan that aims to "create mechanisms to help adapt to climate variability and climate change as well as mechanisms for integrated management of shared resources at the regional level." One key outcome of the Investment Plan is the strengthening of regional research on climate change and its impact on production systems through improving knowledge and by developing and transferring techniques and technologies to adapt to climate change. As discussed below, the USG FTF program will support the ECOWAP plan by working with regional and bilateral partners to develop technologies, disseminate climate-smart soil and water management techniques, build capacity, and share information and expertise.

Proposed Implementation

USAID/WA proposes a two-pronged approach. Climate-smart technologies and practices will be developed and disseminated across the region through their incorporation in the multiple-use services (MUS) component of the soon to be awarded West Africa-Water, Sanitation and Hygiene (WA-WASH)

---

[15] The concept of "climate-smart agriculture" includes a belief that agriculture should sustainably increase productivity and resilience to environmental pressures in a manner that reduces greenhouse gas emissions. (FAO)
[16] Breman, H., B. Fofana & A. Mando; The Lesson of Drente's 'Essen' Soil Nutrient Depletion in Sub-Saharan Africa and Management Strategies for Soil Replenishment; (in Braimoh, A.K. & P.L.G. Vlek; Land Use and Soil Resources; Springer Media, 145 – 166.
[17] 'Zai' are pits or holes in which organic matter is mixed with soil. They concentrate nutrients and water and aid water infiltration and retention. 'Contour bunds' are low stone walls that slow and spread water and prevent soil and organic matter from being washed away

activity. WA-WASH will combine technologies and funding streams (WASH, FTF, and Climate Change Adaptation) in a four-country, highly food insecure area (Mali, Niger, Burkina Faso, and Ghana), with FTF funding supporting programming in Ghana and Mali (potential FTF focus countries), and Global Climate Change Adaptation monies financing interventions in Burkina Faso and Niger. Scaling-up will occur as WA-WASH collaborates with bilateral missions and regional organizations in promoting technology transfer and sharing lessons learned and better management practices in climate-smart agriculture[18]. The aim is to build climate change-resilient agricultural production systems for vulnerable and food-insecure rural households.

Second, to further disseminate climate smart technology, the USG will provide funding to CORAF and CILSS to:

- Assemble and publicize information about these sustainable land management activities, and promote a more focused approach to soil and water management as a foundation of food security in the Sahel;

- Measure the impact of these techniques on livelihoods, production, soil quality, and improved environmental conditions; and

- Assist regional and bilateral partners in making informed choices about which technologies to adopt under specific conditions to improve the resiliency of agricultural systems in the face of climate change.

Because of their established working relationships with national organizations – such as environmental agencies, Ministries of Agriculture, and national agriculture research systems (NARS), CORAF and CILSS are in the best position to disseminate proven climate-smart agriculture technologies to encourage increased production in fragile agro-ecological zones across the region.

Gender

Gender relations differently shape the work of men and women in communities and in institutions, affecting their experience of and response to the impacts of climate change. At the community level, men's and women's different labor patterns and responsibilities are likely to increase the time needed to source water and fuel under conditions of drought and decreasing soil fertility. As these jobs are typically women's work, along with food production and processing, these changes have gendered implications for successful adoption of the climate smart agricultural practices described. Climate changes may also put added pressure on women's access to land in the face of land pressure, both for agricultural land for crop production and for rights to trees and tree products.[19] With Mission support, the WA-WASH program can ensure that context-specific gender analyses are considered in the design of new technologies for soil and water management so as not to add to exacerbate women's time and labor loads.

---

[18] In addition to working with the bilaterals, from a research and development perspective, USAID/WA will continue collaborating with CORAF, CILSS, others national (NARS, Extension Services), and international organizations (IWMI, ICRISAT, African Rice Center. etc.)

[19] Masika, Rachel and Susan Joekes 1997 Environmentally sustainable development and poverty: A gender analysis. Report No.52. Brighton, UK: BRIDGE. http://www.bridge.ids.ac.uk//bridge/reports/re52.pdf

<u>Expected Results</u>

It is anticipated that CORAF and CILSS will work with approximately four to six national organizations to ensure that climate smart techniques are disseminated to the farmer level. The result will be increases in the following:

- Number of climate smart practices disseminated by CORAF and CILSS and adopted by national extension services, environmental agencies, and non-governmental organizations;

- New information tools developed and disseminated at the policy, technical, and farm level; and

- Number of people trained in new practices

The ultimate, long-term result will be an increase in the number of hectares under improved management.

<u>Prioritization</u>

Under a reduced budget scenario, the full range of complementary activities noted above will continue, but in a narrower geographical area within Ghana and Mali.

<u>Sustainability</u>

Agricultural practices that encourage proper soil and water management build long-term sustainability and ensure that investments in fertilizer and seeds are optimized. Long-term studies in the Sahel show that applying fertilizers on weathered soils in the absence of maintaining a soil's organic matter threshold will eventually lead to decreasing responses to fertilizer and ultimately to rendering the soil unproductive. Additionally, although drought resistant seeds can tolerate lower moisture levels, they still require soil moisture to grow. Increasing infiltration of rainfall into the soil and increasing soil organic matter can ensure that more moisture is retained in the soil thus maximizing investments in modified seeds. Overall, proper soil and water management can ensure optimum returns on input investment while increasing overall sustainability of the agricultural system.

2.3.2 Core Investment Area 2: Increased Regional Availability of Improved Agricultural Inputs for Selected Crops

This core investment will be implemented by the Regional Agriculture Office through two mechanisms, which are currently being conceptualized and designed.

<u>Constraints</u>

To address food security needs in West Africa, significant increases in agricultural productivity and food production are required. Yet, FAO data show that cereal yields have stagnated over the last 40 years while yields in other parts of the world have more than doubled and in Asia, tripled[20]. The conclusions of a recent IFPRI/ International Center for Soil Fertility and Agricultural Development (IFDC) fertilizer assessment and an IFPRI analysis indicate that expanded use of improved seeds and fertilizers are critical to raise productivity gains across all food sectors necessary to improve crop yields and overall food

---

[20] FAOSTAT 2010 Report.

security.[21] [22] Productivity gains will depend on these inputs becoming increasingly available and more widely adopted through policy reforms leading to sustainable demand-driven supply structures.

While use of modern inputs is gradually expanding in the region, policy issues, fragmented markets, and weak private sector involvement inhibit their wider availability and use.

The challenges facing the development of a private sector-led seed industry at both the regional and country levels are complex and inter-related. At the country level, risk-averse farmers are unaware of the proven production potential of new seed varieties as there is no well-organized system for research, testing, production, and certification. Furthermore, inadequate marketing and distribution networks limit the amount of improved seed from public institutions and the private sector. Lastly, trade is constrained by outdated and non-uniform quality certification requirements.

Most progress in expanding use of improved varieties has been made with maize and rice where private companies have undertaken multiplication and marketing. Aware of their higher yields and commercial potential, smallholder farmers are increasingly purchasing improved varieties for these crops from private seed dealers involved in production and marketing[23]. Nonetheless, the recent ECOWAP[24] CAADP policy implementation program paper indicates that improved seed production remains extremely low meeting less than 20 percent of current regional demand.[25]

Regional Adaptive Research

The most critical constraint to maximizing the benefits from over 15 years of USAID support to commodity regional research networks through the International Agricultural Research Centers (IARCs) is the inability of farmers to access seed of the high yielding open pollinated varieties developed over the years. For that reason and the Mission's limited funding under the FTF, USAID/WA will initially focus on supporting regional demonstration trials on varieties already released at the bilateral/national level, side by side with hybrids provided by private seed companies, across given agro-ecological zones. The objective is to expose these varieties to farmers for ultimate production and marketing of seed by the private sector. Through these trials jointly supported by bilateral missions under the West Africa Seed Alliance (WASA), farmers have expressed strong interest in improved maize and rice seed in particular. Shortly after approval of the strategy, however, USAID/WA will begin discussions with the Bureau for Food Security (BFS) research team to better integrate the Mission's research investments, especially under CORAF, with the USG's global agriculture research strategy and worked supported by bilateral missions. USAID/WA will also hold discussions on this matter with USDA because of the latter's experience in institutional capacity building for national research institutions and working with the private sector to support research.

Similarly, fertilizer availability and use remains low because of a combination of demand and supply constraints. According to the 2010 IFDC/IFPRI assessment, a highly fragmented market structure and inefficiencies result in large transaction and transport costs. In many countries, fertilizer price controls and subsidies create disincentives for private suppliers to enter the market, hampering the emergence of

[21] IFPRI/IFDC, "Policy Considerations for Improving Regional Fertilizer Markets in West Africa". November 2010.
[22] IFPRI, "Regional Strategic Alternatives for Agricultural-led Growth and Poverty Reduction in West Africa". December 2006.
[23] West African Seeds Alliance, "Seed Production and Constraints in West Africa: An Assessment of the Seed Systems in Ghana, Nigeria, Mali, Niger, Senegal, Burkina Faso, Togo, and Benin". 2009
[24] ECOWAP: ECOWAS Agricultural Program
[25] ECOWAS Commission, Summary Note on Policy Instruments for the Implementation of ECOWAP/CAADP. October 2010.

private sector dealer networks. Compounding the problem, national level quality control is weak and differing quality standards prevent the efficient movement of fertilizer supplies across borders. Lack of market information and forecasting inhibits effective transactions among traders and hinders the integration of a regional fertilizer market.

Strategic Context

All bilateral FTF programs in the region have expressed a need for the USAID/WA to address regional constraints to increasing the availability of agriculture inputs. Similarly, one of ECOWAS' top priorities in the agriculture sector is expanding the use of modern agricultural inputs through a private sector led program. Its strategy to promote intensification on the supply side of agriculture inputs includes boosting local production of fertilizers, organizing the production of bulk blending, promoting the use of natural phosphate produced in the region, promoting the production of improved and certified seeds, and conducting research on the intensification of food crops. On the demand side, ECOWAS proposes to: lower input prices through subsidies (until market expansion limits fertilizer costs by economies of scale), promote distribution networks for agricultural inputs, encourage agricultural finance, and enact tariffs measures and tax incentives at the regional level to encourage intensification.

The USG's strategy for increasing access to fertilizer and improved seed availability will focus on improving the investment environment by removing policy related obstacles impeding private sector investment in fertilizer blending, manufacturing, distribution, and sale in West Africa. Since the wide spread use of subsidies by some national governments represents a significant hurdle to increasing private sector investment in fertilizer, the Mission will support critical policy reform efforts by building the analytical capacity of the recently created Regional Technical Agency for Agriculture and Food (RTAAF) at ECOWAS, and working with agricultural inputs producer associations and other the private sector actors to lobby for needed reforms. Specific fertilizer policy reforms and implementation actions to be targeted include the following: 1) removing tariff and non-tariff controls and taxes, 2) harmonizing pricing and marketing policies as well as fertilizer products; and 3) strengthening quality control systems at the national and regional levels. For seeds, the policy focus will be on the following: 1) ensuring that more countries, in addition to Ghana and Mali, align their national seed laws with the ECOWAS regional regulation on cross-border trade, followed by monitoring implementation; and 2) setting up common quality control standards (SPS).

USAID/WA will work closely with the agricultural inputs industry associations to advocate for policy reform, strengthen commercial networks, and facilitate transactions. The seeds component will initially focus on the maize and rice sectors and, using a model to scale approach, while investigating the advantages of working with other cereals such as sorghum and millet in the future. The maize and rice sectors have exhibited promising growth in the use of improved seed and fertilizer for higher yields; however the production and marketing of improved seed through the private sector need to be expanded.

Proposed Implementation

USAID/WA proposes a focused program with a strong private sector emphasis for rationalizing seed and fertilizer markets and will seek to leverage additional resources through close private sector and development partner coordination with the Africa Development Bank's (AfDB) fertilizer financing facility, IFDC's market development program and AGRA's fertilizer alliance.[26] USAID/WA proposes a program focused on the following main directions:

Improved Policy and Regulatory Environment

More progress has been made in regional marketing of improved **seed** than fertilizer and the passage of the ECOWAS seed law and regulation gives hope for further progress. Ghana and Mali have recently aligned their national laws with the regional regulation, but considerable work must be done to monitor implementation in the region. USAID/WA will continue to work with ECOWAS and regional missions to further the enactment and implementation of the law in member states.

While a regional strategy on **fertilizer** was adopted in 2006, much more needs to be done. USAID/WA will consider supporting activities aimed to harmonize fertilizer prices, eliminate external tariffs, and establish quality standards and key formulations that can be traded regionally. A more coherent market structure and transport reforms are also key elements in reducing fertilizer costs. To this end, the program will be implemented in close collaboration with the Mission's program for increasing trade in agricultural commodities.

Increased Private Sector Production and Distribution of Selected Agricultural Inputs

The Mission will continue to support strengthening commercial relationships at the regional level[27]. Efforts will include facilitating small-scale fertilizer blending and the coordination of trial demonstrations on improved varieties (including hybrids) in joint partnership with private sector international seed and fertilizer companies. Initially, maize and rice will be the primary target crops, followed in later years by sorghum and millet.

The current average yields in maize and irrigated rice in the region are estimated at 1.5 and 2.5 MT/ha respectively. In trial demonstrations under WASA, regional trial demonstrations, private companies and selected farmers have obtained rice yields ranging from 4–8 MT/ha and maize yields of 4–7 MT/ha. There is potential to double current yields in five years with the adoption of improved varieties and fertilizer, increasing agricultural productivity, increasing regional trade and improving food security.

It is worth noting that the results from the proposed trade activities will directly contribute to the above mentioned results. It is estimated that a 10–15 percent reduction in transport costs would result in a 20-30 percent increase in the value of fertilizer traded.[28] It will also be carried out with strong private sector involvement to reduce the current high cost of imported fertilizer associated with transportation and handling inefficiencies in loading and unloading, especially for landlocked states. In partnership with private companies, it is proposed to establish regional fertilizer transit storage warehouses at selected ports corresponding to strategic transport corridors.

Another important regional policy/regulatory matter is **biosafety regulation**, wherein USAID/WA will continue efforts to have ECOWAS/CILSS approve a regional biosafety policy and to support individual countries in passing national biosafety legislation. For over five years, USAID has provided technical

---

[26] In the spirit of increasing coordination and leveraging on existing activities, the Mission will also explore partnerships with other donors and private sector groups. Including the Africa Seed Trade Association, and the Millennium Challenge Corporation which investing in irrigation in Mali, Senegal and Niger.

[27] Selected interventions with both input associations and private sector firms will build on positive lessons learned from the West African Seed Alliance.

[28] Limao, N., and Venables. 2001 "Infrastructure, Geographic Disadvantages, and Transport Costs." World Bank Economic Review 15 (3): 451-79.

assistance to West African regional organizations for the development of a regional policy to harmonize regulations and practices around field trials, risk assessment and commercial cultivation of genetically engineered crops. Following several regional drafting workshops and stakeholder consultations, ECOWAS and CILSS completed a draft regional framework that USAID has determined to be a functional, science-based system for harmonized risk assessments that complements and integrates with national regulatory policies. In parallel, UEMOA, with World Bank funding has been developing a separate regional framework for its member countries that creates a regional approval system much less favorable to development of such crops in West Africa. In late 2009, CILSS/ECOWAS and UEMOA began a process of merging the two systems. The resultant joint regional framework document, which emerged in November 2010, reflects very little of the content of the earlier proposed ECOWAS/CILSS framework, but contains an overarching regional approval system that removes decision-making authority from the national governments. This system will likely make this version of the framework unacceptable to West African countries already implementing biotechnology applications (e.g., Burkina Faso, where 80 percent of cotton, the dominant cash crop, is now genetically engineered) or planning to do so.

USAID/WA interventions in the biosafety sphere will entail support (through CILSS) to a working group between the three major organizations and their member states to revise the current draft regional biosafety framework. USAID/WA will also continue collaboration with USAID/ Washington (EGAT/BFS and BFS/ART) in the future since we do not have a technical specialist in this domain. The objectives of this effort will be as follows: (i) to have an acceptable regional biosafety framework approved by the end of 2011; (ii) to support individual countries in collaboration with the bilateral missions to harmonize their biosafety regulations with the regional framework; (iii) to train individuals at regional workshops on subjects related to biosafety; and (iv) to develop and disseminate information materials related to biosafety and biotechnology.

Gender

The high participation of women in agriculture, estimated by the World Bank and International Labor Organization (ILO) to average about 45 percent of the agricultural labor force across Sub-Saharan Africa, makes them an important focus of input markets, as their preferences will be critical for driving demand for new seed varieties and applications of other inputs. The example of NERICA rice and its successful adoption in the region is a case of how attention to the preferences of women farmers can not only increase adoption rates, but also demonstrates how adoption of improved varieties increases women's income and yields.[29]

To replicate this type of success, USAID/WA, in its institutional support to CORAF, will encourage the strengthening of policies on participatory breeding programs to ensure the inclusion of women and to encourage National Agriculture Research Systems (NARS) to do the same. According to a recent report on a gender training given to CORAF in December 2010, NARS staff reported the national institutions do not have written gender strategies and leadership by CORAF could catalyze this effort.

The Mission will continue work to collect and analyze data about women agro-dealers as well as data about the preferences of women as seed and input consumers. Beyond the understanding that women tend to buy fewer inputs in lower quantities, there is limited data gaps about gendered patterns of seed and input purchases, especially in a context of expanding regional markets. The challenge is to develop successful communication strategies and identify appropriate communication channels to communicate

---

[29] A. R. Agboh-Noameshie, F. M. Kinkingninhoun-Medagbe, and A. Aliou 2008 "Gendered Impact of NERICA Adoption on Farmers' Production and Income in Central Benin" No. 11. In Advancing Technical Change in African Agriculture. http://purl.umn.edu/52082.

to women and resource poor farmers the value to them of fertilizer and/or improved seeds use to enhance food security. Marketing messages that emphasize time, resources, and nutritional benefits, as well as the demonstrated increase in yields for home consumption needs to be developed. Providing training and capacity building to enhance women's participation in agro-dealer networks or to develop a new network of women agro-dealers will help to spur growth in the seed and fertilizer industries.

Expected Results

The success of the proposed interventions will be measured by increases in the volume and value of sales of improved quality seeds for selected food staples and fertilizer above the current levels. A 2010 WASA project assessment concluded that in eight countries surveyed, the average amount of improved maize and rice seed sold was only approximately 12 percent (10,700 MT) and 13 percent (11,000 MT) respectively of the demand. USAID/WA expects to raise this figure to at least 25 percent (22,300 MT for maize and 21,150 MT for rice) in five years. The Mission plans to achieve this by strengthening at least 50 percent of the National Seed Trade Associations so that they can effectively advocate for the seed industry. A comparable number of local seed companies in focus countries will also be strengthened in financial and business management. In the case of fertilizer, the ECOWAP summary implementation document and other sources indicate that current fertilizer consumption in the region is 1.2 million metric tons (approximately 9-10 kg/ha). In five years, USAID expects to raise the volume of fertilizer sales by between 10-15 percent in 8 selected countries.

Based on rice and maize yields in regional trials (4-7 MT/ha and 4-8 MT/ha, respectively), a 12 percent improved maize yield and a 13 percent improved rice seed yield are expected to result in an increase in maize production of 2.14 million MT and increase in rice production of 133,000 MT. On the same basis, if the amount of improved maize and rice seed sold meets 25 percent of the expected result, it will translate into increased production of 4.46 million MT of maize and 256,000 MT of rice. This will be a significant production increase – especially if intensive production is practiced – given the current regional average maize and rice yields of only 1.5 and 2.5 MT/ha.

In the case of fertilizer, the application of 1 kg of fertilizer helps to restore soil fertility, replenish nutrients in depleted soils, and can potentially generate 10-15 kg of grain. Therefore, a 10 percent increase in fertilizer use means the application of an additional 120,000 MT of fertilizer, which will result in an increase in grain production of 1.2 million MT.

On the policy front, during the strategy period, USAID/WA will assist ten West African countries in adopting national biosafety regulations, and all 15 ECOWAS member states in adopting national seed policy regulations.

Prioritization

Both the seeds and fertilizer subsectors of the agricultural inputs program will be implemented through public-private sector alliance mechanisms. USAID/WA narrowed the main directions of activity from four to two, selecting those that require limited financial resources but are considered critical for the successful functioning of private sector-led seeds and fertilizer industries. USAID/WA will leverage additional resources from bilateral Missions, which are already funding over fifty percent of the WASA budget. Other donors and private sector partners, including the European Union, Pioneer, and AGRA, will fund bulk fertilizer purchases, transit storage warehouses at selected ports, and strengthening of national seed trade associations and agricultural input dealers. USAID/WA has a strong comparative advantage in working at the regional level, has long collaborated with and supported regional organizations, and played the leading role in mobilizing other donors. With this in mind, the Mission believes that other alliance partners will fund the more expensive activities, especially given the awareness that has been raised in the region on the importance of agricultural inputs in raising productivity.

Highest priority will be given to activities on the policy/regulatory environment and the private sector, particularly for the fertilizer sub-sector, cutting funding for capacity-building for input associations and dealers. Policy harmonization will facilitate cross-border trade by private investors, while fertilizer blending under the private sector direction will lead to (i) reduced transport costs because of proximity to the farms and use of local materials as fertilizer fillers; (ii) provision of custom fertilizer formulations; and (iii) more efficient fertilizer use. Since some countries in the region are already investing in fertilizer blending, these countries can serve as pilots for this endeavor.

<u>Sustainability</u>

The major challenge to sustainability will be ensuring that the private sector assumes responsibility and ownership for private sector-led market development for seeds and fertilizers. Program interventions proposed will develop and support private sector strengthening through training, information exchange, policy advocacy, and developing strategic industry alliances to work towards common business goals and growth of the seed and fertilizer industries. These activities will create an enabling environment for industry growth through policy analysis, dialogue, and reform ensuring industry stakeholders have a voice in debate. The key assumption for program sustainability is that the dynamic created from developing the mutual interests of both farmers and supplier/dealers will be sustained through the commercial relationships and partnerships forged in a more connected commercial environment and coherent and integrated market structure.

<u>Increased Regional Trade in Staple Foods (Intermediate Result 2)</u>

Over the past decade, West Africa has become more dependent on food imports while its own food production has not kept pace with the region's growing population. West African food production is undermined by a number of trade- and transportation-related barriers. As a result, West African markets are fragmented – weakening the incentives to invest in more productive agricultural technologies and contributing to a lack of availability and price volatility of staple foods. The primary constraints to greater regional trade in staple foods are inefficient transportation, trade barriers, and poorly performing regional markets for these products. In response to these trade issues and under an overarching core investment area – Increased Regional Trade in Key Agricultural Commodities, USAID/WA will undertake activities in three main areas: *Improved Competitiveness of Transport and Logistics; Reduced Legal and Regulatory Barriers to Trade;* and *Improved Efficiency of Regional Market Transactions.*

2.3.3   Core Investment Area 3: Increased Regional Trade in Key Agricultural Commodities

This core investment will be implemented by the Regional Trade and Investment Office (RTIO). Activities similar in size and scope are currently being successfully implemented through two mechanisms. USAID/WA is in the process of streamlining these activities to better match the FTF objectives. However, the longer-term plan is that, with the conclusion of the three current activities, a single mechanism will be designed in keeping with the sub-activities as described below.

Improve the Competitiveness of the Transportation and Logistics Sector

USAID/WA will support work in this area with two sources of funding, focusing FTF resources for transport/logistics interventions on the potential FTF focus countries of Ghana, Mali, and Senegal, and using other Economic Growth funds to support similar work in non-FTF focus countries in the region. In practical terms, this means that the Mission's FTF program will concentrate on transport corridors that link Ghana to Burkina Faso and Mali on through to Senegal.

West African trucks are older, cover less ground, at lower speeds, with less of a payload than anywhere else in the world. The poor state of trucking is a result of systemic disincentives to invest in transportation. There are a number of national government policies and regional practices that hinder more efficient trucking. Transportation agreements limit backhaul and discourage investment. The informality of the sector encourages bribery at borders and along trade routes. There is also a lack of competition built into the practices through which ports allocate trucks to shipments. These factors result in high transportation costs for cereals and livestock. A recent study that focused three West African countries found that transport and logistics costs accounted for approximately 59 percent and 18 percent respectively of end market price for maize and livestock.

To lower the cost of food staples, West Africa will need to improve the competitiveness of their transport and logistics sector. A key element to lower costs and encourage investment will be advancing a reform agenda for the transport and logistics sector. Rwanda's experience in deregulating trucking suggests that hauling rates could drop by 30 percent if regional liberalization of transit trucking were to occur. This will include continuing efforts to reduce road harassment of truckers by officials along West Africa's trade and transit corridors.

USAID/WA will also support the creation of a regional transportation network dedicated to better management and increasing the incentives for informal-sector truckers to adopt more formal and efficient approaches. One tool in this strategy will be a web-based, freight-exchange system such as the one currently under development in Burkina Faso, a country linked by the major corridors of interest to Ghana and Mali. The exchange tool would be used to lower costs of transport by increasing logistical efficiency in linking freight to trucks. For informal sector shippers of cereals, livestock, and other agricultural outputs and inputs the system will provide more options for finding backhaul and provide a free-market alternative to the system of quota and queuing-based allocation of freight that is so inefficient. To increase impact per assistance dollar, USAID/WA will prioritize work in countries where initial startup investments have been made. USAID/WA is working on transport corridors that link Ghana to Burkina Faso and Mali on through to Senegal. Bribes and delays, transport costs, and price differentials for staple foods between producing and consuming areas are relatively high along this corridor and therefore are offer an opportunity for improvement.

Reduced Legal and Regulatory Barriers to Trade

Traders continue to face substantial barriers to moving staple foods across borders. Such barriers include seasonal bans, excessive tariffs and fees, customs procedures, and SPS requirements. Often, legitimate health issues such as control of aflatoxin contamination become a justification to require an informal payment. Misapplication of such measures increases transaction costs, creates uncertainty, delays shipments and, thus, constrains regional trade. For example, the costs of official trade and regulatory measures for maize traded from central Ghana to southern Burkina Faso have been estimated to add over 30 percent to farm gate prices.[30]

---

[30] "Agricultural Trade Policy and Transport in West Africa," West Africa Trade Hub Report. January 2011. Page 3.

USAID/WA will reduce legal and regulatory barriers to trade in staple foods through more consistent implementation of the provision of ECOWAS's free trade agreement. This will entail streamlining customs practices and developing regionally harmonized grades and standards for key staple foods and assist the private sector comply with legitimate health and safety requirements.

Customs clearance in many West African countries entails long delays, even for goods that should require minimum clearance times. Under ECOWAS and UEMOA regulations, agricultural goods and livestock are duty free, and along with other unprocessed goods and handcrafts, do not require Certificates of Origin, although SPS certification is required. However, depending on the country of export, traders may need additional documentation. Mali, for example, requires authorization from provincial governors for livestock exports, along with completion of an "Intent to Export" form. Once traders have all necessary documentation, customs clearance should be routine and fast. The Mission will undertake training of customs officials on the appropriate procedures for clearing regional agricultural goods.

USAID/WA will also assist ECOWAS and national customs authorities to establish a Joint Border Community Development Committee with private sector participation. The Mission will include a formal mechanism for joint planning by relevant stakeholders to create border environment where stakeholders can function together in a more transparent manner to implement regional trade protocols. Key to achieving this goal and an important outcome of these activities is a better-informed trade community, including both the public and private sectors. Accurate information on trading rules – for both traders and officials – is a main ingredient to consistent application of laws and regulations. However, knowledge and information alone are insufficient when there is no oversight or checks and balances in a system corroded by corruption. Achieving adherence to the rules also requires cooperation among diverse parties with competing interests and a commitment to a common goal. The basic practices required for this context, however, are not in place in the border areas.

To summarize, the primary activities to reduce trade regulatory barriers will be: making rules and regulations publicly available; ensuring ECOWAS and private sector/civil society representation at key borders; and capacity-building for public and private sector representatives to implement trade agreements. This intervention will begin as a pilot program at three to four borders along corridors strategically important to regional agricultural trade. Fuller implementation of trade agreements will reduced delays and losses routinely experienced by agricultural traders in transit, especially in the case of livestock. Traders will also benefit from the reduced paperwork and related fees (formal and informal) and more certainty due to better and more consistent application of rules for regional agricultural trade. USAID/WA is working in capitals and along transport corridors and borders that link Ghana to Burkina Faso and Mali on through to Senegal. If fully funded, USAID/WA will invest in additional transport corridors, capitals, and borders; examples would include work improve the implementation of the ECOWAS regional policy regime in Liberia. These are important countries from a food security perspective, but would require sufficient initial investments.

Improved Efficiency of Regional Market Transactions

The Mission will improve the efficiency of regional market transactions for key staple foods by building the capacity of regional private sector organizations and market institutions. Producers, traders, and buyers rely on limited, largely traditional linkages to other actors in their value chains and on relatively weak producers' and traders' organizations that fail to build region-wide linkages. It is difficult to quantify the cost of poor linkages, however, a Mission project – through a number of low cost market facilitation efforts aimed at informing sellers of the requirements of buyers – managed to increase live cattle sales between markets in Burkina Faso and Nigeria by $10.4 million annually through additional sales of 200 head per week.[31]

USAID/WA will train a network of market facilitators in key markets; these actors will provide direct support to regional transactions. Experience suggests that there can be a large return on such intermediation, especially where knowledge of buyer requirements in a distant but potentially large market is lacking. The Mission will support regular buyer-seller events, in collaboration with actors that already do this on an occasional basis. Such events have the potential to substantially increase volumes of transactions. Sustainability of these planned interventions will depend largely on building leading value-chain specific regional associations. In certain instances, such as cereals, there has not been a regional cereal producer's association, so program efforts must first ensure the creation of one (using the model of the East African Grain Council). Capacity-building will increase the association's ability to inform policy formulation (on issues such as SPS standards), engage more effectively in trade facilitation, improving access to credit, and achieving greater gender equity in the agricultural sector. Efforts to increase access to finance for actors engaged in regional transactions involving food staple commodities are also an important form of facilitation – including actions to alleviate constraints relating to both conventional credit issues and international payments – are also an important component of trade facilitation.

Although a great deal of progress has been made in West Africa in developing better systems for disseminating trade information, it remains difficult for producers and traders – especially ones operating on a small scale – to obtain timely and reliable information on prices, bids, offers, and quality in distant markets, especially over regional borders. This factor contributes to the high degree of dispersion of prices for a given food staple crop across the region.[32] Moreover, differences in the means of operation, objectives, and quality of information have led to the existence of separate private and public market information systems (MIS) in most countries; these MIS have rarely collaborated with one another, leading to confusion and duplication of effort.

Even in the absence of functional private or public MIS, there is evidence of large benefits from the availability of cell phone technology for agricultural sector actors. For example, the use of cell phones in Niger enabled traders to search over a larger number of markets, leading to a reduction in price dispersion across markets of at least 6.4 percent and reduced inter-annual price variation by 10 percent.[33] The economic gains from the introduction of cell phones include 3-4 percent reductions in millet prices for households, enabling them to consume the grain for an additional eight-twelve days.

In order for reduced price dispersion and volatility and lower consumer prices to benefit entire agro-climatic zones, there is a need for a regional MIS that provides equally reliable, timely, and user-friendly information. Such MIS would enable traders to query and compare prices in and receive bids and offers from other countries. USAID/WA will support MIS based on cell phone technology on a multi-country basis as a means to reducing prices and price dispersion and volatility, which should in turn increase intra-regional trade.

---

[31] USAID/WA Agribusiness and Trade Promotion (ATP) Project, Annual Progress Report: October 2008-September 2009, p. 25. For comparison purposes, total annual cattle sales in the 13 markets in six West African countries where ATP measures trade flows come to about $240 million.

[32] See, e.g., the iso-price maps contained in "Agricultural Trade Policy and Transport in West Africa," report prepared by CARANA for USAID/WA, January 2011.

[33] Jenny C. Aker, "Does Digital Divide or Provide? The Impact of Cell Phones on Grain Markets in Niger," University of California, Berkeley, February 2008. She also found that during the food crisis in Niger in 2005, price dispersion among markets in food-crisis regions was 20 percent higher than in non-crisis regions; only 24 percent of the former were in regions with cell phone coverage, as compared to 83 percent in the latter regions.

USAID/WA will focus the work on Improved Efficiency of Regional Market Transactions on the aforementioned cereal and livestock value chains and concentrate along the priority transport corridors connecting Tema and Ouagadougou and Dakar and Bamako (and important trunk roads for the transport of those commodities).

Gender

Women are recognized to be actively engaged in regional trade across West Africa[34], although precise figures are not available. A recent USAID study noted that "interviews with traders in the field show that there is more trade occurring than what is officially registered. For example, roughly 2400 female traders (clients of a MFI dedicated to providing financial services to poor women) perform a range of trading activities in the informal sector." There are significant gaps on the extent of women's involvement in regional trade relative to men, about the types of commodities traded, and on the impact the income they earn on economic growth generally.[35] These data holes make it difficult to develop evidence-based trade-off analyses of the impact of investments on, e.g., women's income and/or children's nutrition. However, a focus on improving conditions for cross border trade in general will disproportionately benefit women who dominate the informal trade and suffer particularly severely from the corruption and harassment that frequently afflict petty agricultural traders.

Reports on women entrepreneurs in the region have consistently identified that women face challenges in moving out of informal trading into larger enterprises. They report needing more effective channels for accessing information on the rules of commerce in the region, and mechanisms to help them overcome other barriers to expanded participation, such as access to credit, exchanging money, police and border harassment, and high communications and transport costs.[36]

Expected Results

The overall indicator of success in these endeavors will be the value and volume of intra-regional trade in food staple value chains, principally cereals and livestock, along the where USAID/WA's program is active.

Analytically, the Regional Strategic Analysis and Knowledge Support System (ReSAKSS) scenario to reduce West Africa's poor by 46 million people assumes both a substantial increase in regional trade and productivity improvements for staple foods and livestock. These two changes combined would lead to an estimated doubling of agricultural exports from West Africa, with regional agricultural exports reaching $22.1 billion, versus $10.6 billion under a "business as usual" scenario. Half of this increase of the doubling (50 percent) would come from improvements in market access and reduction in the associated costs to trade.

---

[34] Orozco, Manuel 2006 "West African Financial Flows and Opportunities for People and Small Businesses." Prepared by Carana Corporation. Washington, D.C.: USAID, page 14.

[35] United Nations Economic Commission for Africa (UNECA), African Union Commission (AUC) and African Development Bank (AfDB) 2010 "Gender and Intra African Trade: The Case of West Africa" (Chapter 12) in Assessing Regional Integration in Africa VI: Enhancing Intra African Trade. Addis Ababa: UN Economic Commission for Africa;

[36] United Nations Economic Commission for Africa (UNECA), African Union Commission (AUC) and African Development Bank (AfDB) 2010 "Gender and Intra African Trade: The Case of West Africa" (Chapter 12) in Assessing Regional Integration in Africa VI: Enhancing Intra African Trade. Addis Ababa: UN Economic Commission for Africa; Nathan-MSI Group 2001 "West Africa Businesswomen's Network (WABNET) and West African Women's Association Secretariat. Washington, D.C.: USAID.

Looking specifically at transactions costs, a study by USAID of the trade corridor from Tema (Ghana) to Ouagadougou found that trade and transport along this corridor costs three times more than and takes two to three times as long as containerized cargo traveling comparable distances in the U.S. Bulk cargo transport is even less efficient. A reduction of the average trip duration from Ouagadougou to Tema of 7.5 to 5 days would decrease costs by between 2.5 and 10 percent. Using rough averages, a reduction of 10 percent in transport costs will enable approximately 20 percent growth in trade.

<u>Higher Level Expected Result</u>

USAID/WA will target a doubling of regional trade in key commodities over five years. Part of this expected doubling will come from reducing the deadweight costs of trade and transportation and other market inefficiencies. Based on current analysis, USAID/WA expects that a 10 to 15 percent reduction in trade and transport costs is achievable within the five-year implementation period and a 50 percent reduction in transport costs within ten years.

Successful implementation will have direct impacts on consumer prices, production, incomes, and consumption of the targeted staple foods. The analysis of the variance of supply and demand for agricultural commodities suggests that for a reduction in transaction costs on the order of 10 percent of farm gate prices would yield a 4 percent increase in production. Since this likely represents the full cash income of the impacted producers, the analysis concludes that they would experience a similar 4 percent increase in income.

Similarly, the analysis concludes that the same 4 percent increase in production would likely result in an 8 percent drop in end-market prices and a resulting increase in disposable incomes for end-market consumers of approximately 7 percent. Such a change would have a substantial positive impact on urban livelihoods.

Other Expected Results:

- 10 percent decline in hours of travel time between key pairs of regional markets

- 10 percent decline in cost per 1,000 kilometers of road transport for cereals and livestock

- $12 million in finance mobilized for regional trade transactions in maize and livestock (cumulatively over five years)

- 20 percent reduction in the average variation among prices in major markets for cereals and livestock

<u>Prioritization</u>

With respect to prioritization within the area of *Improved Efficiency of Regional Market Transactions*, USAID/WA would accord the highest priority to direct market facilitation efforts, which the Mission's experience has shown are particularly cost effective and successful. Second order of priority would go to work on market information systems, which show great promise in linking dispersed traders to markets and reducing price dispersion. Lowest priority would be given to interventions on access to finance and expanded use of standards and grades. The former have proven particularly difficult to implement at the regional level, where payments issues conspire with all the usual problems in attracting lenders to agricultural projects. In the case of the latter, activities on standards and grades (including

SPS) would have to be left to other USG agencies, especially USDA, which has long conducted training on this subject (albeit often with funding from USAID).

<u>Sustainability</u>

The major challenge to sustainability will be ensuring the private sector assumes ownership of a regional trade and transportation reform agenda. The private sector must be capable of advancing this agenda without relying on continuous donor assistance. Effective advocacy requires practical analysis and dialogue with officials that focus public debate on actionable outcomes. USAID/WA will build strategic industry alliances that are financially sustainable and train members to be effective in working with regional governments. Program sustainability will rely ultimately on demonstrating to stakeholder that investing in advocacy improves companies' ability to compete adds to the net welfare of West Africans and is politically viable for officials to undertake.

<u>Increased Capacity of Regional Agricultural Sector Actors (Intermediate Result 3)</u>

As a support Intermediate Result, the Mission seeks to facilitate greater success under *Improved Agricultural Sustainable Productivity* and *Increased Regional Trade in Staple Foods* by addressing critical institutional capacity issues, which hinder the ability of select partners to adequately address food security in the region. This is part of the Mission's commitment to promote African leadership as well as ensure greater sustainability through strengthen of African lead organizations.

2.3.4 Core Investment Area 4: Increased Capacity of Regional Agricultural Sector Actors

This core investment will be implemented by the Regional Agriculture Office through a specific capacity building activity (Africa LEAD) as well as activities carried out through Implementation Letters with CILSS and CORAF. A secondary focus of capacity-building activities will be professional/trade and civil society organizations that, among other things advocate for improved policy on the part of these formal regional organizations

> **Implementing ECOWAP: What is RTAAF?**
>
> Implementing the ECOWAS common agricultural policy (ECOWAP) requires a coherent institutional framework, reliable fundraising mechanisms, and operational programs. In 2009 stakeholders – including member states and representatives of civil society institutions – adopted the "Regional Partnership Compact for Implementation of ECOWAP". To implement ECOWAP, they decided to create and finance a Regional Technical Agency for Agriculture and Food (RTAAF).

<u>Constraints and Rationale</u>

Healthy and robust African regional institutions and civil society are critical to the success of the ECOWAS/CAADP Regional Partnership for Implementation of ECOWAP. Regional governmental agencies and institutions as well as non-governmental and civil society organizations must ensure that investments and regional policy are driven by sound analysis to promote increased regional trade and agricultural productivity. At present, there are only a handful of mature and institutionally robust regional organizations that have the technical capacity, leverage, and scope to effectively advocate on behalf of their stakeholders. Capacity building on a number of levels will be needed within the implementing organizations, and, more broadly, in non-government and private sector stakeholder organizations. USAID/WA is currently undertaking an institutional assessment to analyze key organizations in the region. Based on the results of this assessment, the Mission will craft a focused capacity building program that targets a few select organizations.

Strategic Context

Through FTF, USAID/WA, which has provided major support to developing the ECOWAP Implementation Plan, will continue to provide assistance in capacity building to ensure its implementation. The Mission is strongly committed to African leadership and ownership. As such, it will support a variety of programs/activities that ensure the selected regional entities develop full capacity to undertake their own organizational functions. In time, the program could develop into a regional platform for training and skills development of African organizations.

Both public and private sector regional institutions are essential to the success of this program. Public sector intergovernmental organizations to be supported include the newly created RTAAF, CILSS (including AGHYRMET – it's climate and agro data agency), and CORAF. These are the main technical bodies for agricultural development in West Africa with mandates directly linked to the regional implementation of ECOWAP.

Proposed Implementation

USAID/WA will work with the selected regional inter-governmental organizations to improve and strengthen their management and financial systems as well as their information management and analysis capabilities to manage and monitor regional agriculture and food security program included in the ECOWAP. Illustrative activities include the following:

- Strengthen AARA's ability to finance, implement, monitor, and evaluate the ECOWAP/CAADP Implementation Program.

- Strengthen AARA's ability to ensure that women as well as men participate fully in and have access to ECOWAP programs.

- Improve CILSS technical and managerial capacity to implement their food and climate smart agriculture/natural resources management programs including: capacity to coordinate with national governments and regional organizations on food security and natural resources programs; and strengthen financial management systems capacity to work with international research and other regional organizations.

- Improve CILSS early warning information system to include nutritional and climate change information as well as expand the system to all ECOWAS countries as well as Chad and Mauritania.

- Improve CORAF's technical and managerial capacity to implement their climate smart agriculture research programs and to better coordinate with national governments and regional organizations on climate smart agricultural research programs; and strengthen CORAF's financial management system to work with national, regional and international research organizations.

- Support harmonization of the West African Regional Vulnerability Assessment Mechanism to better reflect the international World Food Program (WFP)/FAO framework.

Gender

Many West African regional organizations such as ECOWAS, CORAF, and CILSS have already taken steps to develop policies on gender equality in recent years. The challenge they face is integrating the principles into their implementation efforts. USAID/WA will ensure that the programs it supports in these organizations will take these policies into account, specifically to promote the hiring and retention of qualified women to institutional position, to include both women and men in relevant training and capacity building programs as well as ensure that women as well as men have access to and benefit from program resources. The Mission will support the development, if needed, of a policy on gender equality in the new ECOWAP Implementation Agency and will determine what resources can be offered to ensure that the policy principles are integrated throughout its activities. This might include supporting a position of a gender advisor or providing technical assistance to the new organization. In addition, the Mission will support ECOWAP to improve its collection and use of gender-relevant data.

Expected Results

The USG's proposed approach will lead to more robust African organizations better able to lead efforts to address regional food security and climate change issues. Due to the role that regional organizations play, this, in turn, will increase the overall success of Mission efforts under the first three core investment areas. Lastly, with the capacity building program on technical, managerial and financial issues the most important regional institutions (CILSS/CORAF and ECOWAS) will be able to better perform and implement the policies, new technologies and good governance.
By 2015, CILSS will be able to achieve the following:

- Improve food security early warning system in all 15 West African countries (i.e., ECOWAS member states) plus Chad and Mauritania.

- Include nutritional assessment information in the food security system in all West African countries plus Chad and Mauritania.

- Improve regional food security reports, with better information on markets, prices, crop flows from surplus to deficit areas and nutrition assessments.

- Implement the new Vulnerability Assessment Mechanism in all West African countries

- Improve the managerial and financial capacity of its staff.

CORAF will be able to achieve the following by that same year:

- Better coordinate with the National Agricultural Research Systems and the existing CGIAR centers in the region.

- Improve the managerial and financial capacities of its staff.

- Strengthen the capacities of 500 producers in ten countries to respond to their needs, including with respect to technology, input sources, credit, and markets.

- Release at least ten new market-responsive varieties in West Africa (selected from among, rice, millet, sorghum, cassava, yam, and cowpea).

- Assist at least 400 producers groups in ten countries to adopt improved inland valley management practices for multiple cropping.

At ECOWAS, the new RTAAF will have successfully begun to fulfill its mandate, with a staff adequately trained on managerial and financial issues, enabling to play the public sector role in implementing the regional ECOWAP/CAADP Investment plan and to approve the new regional biosafety regulations.

<u>Prioritization</u>

With respect to prioritization among these activities, USAID/WA will concentrate on providing support to the establishment of ECOWAS's RTAAF (including three staff members), institutional support and capacity building to CORAF (including three staff members), and institutional support to CILSS, with a concentration on early warning systems.

3. COORDINATION AND MANAGEMENT

3.1 WHOLE OF GOVERNMENT

Because of the broad nature (geographic and otherwise) of its programs and regional support responsibilities, the USG's Whole of Government approach is equally broad. In order to capitalize on existing USG efforts, USAID/WA has developed a multi-pronged approach towards Whole of Government. This includes:

- **Bilateral Coordination:** Using the mechanism of an advisory board, the Mission will continue collaborating with bilateral USAID missions as it implements this strategy. Close coordination will be required for core investment areas focused on inputs and improving regional trade.

- **USAID/Food for Peace (FFP) and Office of Foreign Disaster Assistance (OFDA):** USAID/FFP, from its regional office in Dakar, manages both emergency and non-emergency programming. The latter, which has more obvious synergies with the objectives of FTF, aims at addressing the underlying causes of poverty and malnourishment in Burkina Faso, Chad, Liberia, Mali, Mauritania, Niger, Senegal, and Sierra Leone, three of which – Liberia, Mali, and Senegal – have bilateral missions with which USAID/WA coordinates its activities. Specific interventions under FFP non-emergency programming in the region include productivity enhancement through irrigation, improved seed, and better agricultural practices; farmer field schools to teach, for example, use of organic fertilizer; microcredit; repair/construction of feeder roads and animal watering points; literacy programs; support to extension services; and on farm storage to reduce post-harvest losses. Collaboration between FFP and FTF activities could take the form of the FFP-support programs working on these basic needs at the village level, enabling smallholders and their associations to eventually "graduate" to larger scale, more business- and trade-oriented interventions under FTF. Although such a transition is more obviously the province of bilateral USAID programming under FTF, to the extent that FFP non-emergency program beneficiaries live in border regions or would otherwise benefit from increased access to cross-border markets, graduation from FFP programs to inclusion in regionally focused activities under USAID/WA is a realistic possibility. OFDA also conducts a number of activities in West Africa relating to food security and nutrition that suggest opportunities for collaboration with USAID/WA. For example, in FY 2010, it supported WFP to conduct a baseline assessment of regional markets in the Western Basin of the region (including Senegal), in an effort better to understand trade routes and trader behavior. In addition, since FY 2006, it has supported HKI in developing models for prevention and treatment of malnutrition in Burkina Faso, Mali, and Niger.

- **Non-Presence Country (NPC) Embassies:** USAID will work closely with U.S. Embassies to engage them in advocating with national governments for the implementation of critical regional policies. USAID/WA has program managers in select NPCs (Burkina Faso, Niger, Chad, and Mauritania) to ensure effective coordination with the Department of State in implementing activities in these countries. These on-the-ground managers have greatly improved coordination.

- **Peace Corps:** While USAID/WA is not well placed to work with the ultra-poor in the region, Peace Corps is. USAID will provide funding to Peace Corps to support volunteers in non-presence countries in West Africa that are working with communities to improve production, marketing, and better utilization of available resources at the grass roots level. Activities will focus on crops and commodities traditionally controlled and produced primarily by women. Peace Corps Volunteers (PCVs) will work with local governmental extension services to develop training programs, reinforce and train local trainers, establish farmers field schools, establish community gardens, and help local associations access funding through micro-finance institutions for projects requiring capital investment which are immediate priorities for community food security.

- **U.S. Department of Agriculture (USDA)**:   USDA and USAID/WA have a long history of collaboration. USDA, through such services as the Foreign Agricultural Service (FAS) and the Animal and Plant Inspection Service (APHIS) focuses on trade capacity building, biotechnology, food safety, animal health, and SPS issues. To date, collaboration with USDA has centered on training programs, including Cochran fellowships on such matters as raising livestock and on workshops on such matters as SPS standards. Under this strategy, such cooperation will be broadened to include such areas of USDA expertise as seed certification, grades and standards, warehouse management, and agricultural statistics. Synergies exist where USAID work on warehouse receipt systems would complement FAS programming on warehouse management. With respect to agricultural statistics, USAID/WA has held discussions with USDA's National Agricultural Statistics Service (NASS) concerning the possibility of them providing capacity-building for agencies in the region producing agricultural statistics (e.g., CILSS). Collaboration is also possible with national-level projects under USDA's Food for Progress, where such programs exist in border regions or support beneficiaries for whom increased access to cross-border markets would improve their food security and increase regional trade in food staples.

- **U.S. Commercial Service** and **EXIM Bank:** USAID/WA will coordinate with both organizations as they can facilitate importation of modern trucks for the *Increased Regional Trade's* transport program.

- **U.S. Department of State, U.S. Trade Representatives (USTR) and the Department of Commerce:** USAID/WA will coordinate with these organizations, which will continue to be vital allies in raising with senior officials the border-related issues and their impact on food security. USTR, in particular, has long maintained a keen interest in the Mission's programs aimed at enhancing trade both within the region and between the region and the rest of the world. Its interest has concentrated on matters connected to the Mission's activities to enhance exports under the African Growth and Opportunity Act and its programming in cotton-producing African countries that have raised the issue of U.S. domestic subsidies in the context of the World Trade Organization.

- **Millennium Challenge Corporation (MCC):** MCC has investment in the port in Benin and road construction in Burkina Faso and is planning infrastructure development and other interventions during the strategy period that will complement USAID/WA's trade and transport activities. MCC has also made substantial investments in irrigation in Burkina Faso, Mali, and Senegal. Even though USAID/WA will not be supporting irrigation activities during the strategy period, it will seek to maximize the benefits of MCC investments by targeting some of the regional adaptive seed trials under the Core Investment Area on agricultural inputs toward selected MCC irrigation sites.

- **U.S. Geological Survey (USGS):** At an activity level, USAID/WA works closely with USGS in efforts to promote climate-smart agriculture. This is a continuation of an existing relationship, which uses satellite image analysis and other tools to map long-term agricultural and environmental change in Sahelian woodland ecosystems and the Upper Guinean Forest ecosystem. In the future, plans are to continue using the same analytic tools to track change in key Sahelian sites and in other agro-ecologic zones with FTF investments to measure the impact of USAID programs. Additionally, with USGS, the Mission plans to identity and document sustainable land use practices, which can be promoted to encourage climate change adaptation and livelihood resiliency.

- **U.S. African Development Fund (USADF):** The United States African Development Foundation (USADF) supports small-scale projects on agricultural production, processing, and marketing for marginalized community groups, cooperatives, agriculture producer groups, and small scale enterprises in nine West African countries. These investments help achieve food security objectives of creating jobs, improving incomes, and increasing available food supplies at the farmer and household level. As with FFP and USDA, collaboration is possible with these USADF activities, where they exist in border regions or support beneficiaries for whom increased access to cross-border markets would improve their food security and increase regional trade in food staples.

3.2   MONITORING AND EVALUATION

USAID/WA is establishing a robust regional Monitoring and Evaluation system to provide timely and high-quality data and analysis on progress toward results of its program. This information will be used to advance priority setting in the FTF initiative as well as to identify successful strategies and fine-tune implementation. The M&E system will provide reports on achievements, challenges, and lessons learned to a variety of stakeholders. It will also be set up to track a number of critical indicators of progress in the programs. The RAO M&E Specialist and Mission M&E Specialist will set up the monitoring and evaluation systems, at both Mission and partner level, to track and report M&E information across the FTF program. The M&E team will:

- Ensure that all relevant core indicators are included within the system as well as ensure that definitions, baselines, and targets are established.

- Assist all partners to develop and maintain sound M&E systems.

- Ensure collection and analysis of information for routine reporting (e.g. quarterly/annual reports).

- Provide assistance to staff in planning M&E efforts, designing and managing program analyses, evaluations and special studies, and disseminating evaluative information to all stakeholders.

- Ensure that, where appropriate, all indicators and data collected and tracked are disaggregated by gender.

The Mission's FTF M&E system will be comprised of several integrated elements that will meet the planning, management and reporting needs of Mission managers. The principle M&E elements include:

1. Required FTF Indicators: The West Africa mission will track and report on all FTF required indicators that are consistent with the Mission's FTF program and for which data are available on a regional basis. The Mission anticipates collecting data for and reporting on 22 of the 25 required FTF indicators[37].

2. Performance Indicators: Due to the regional nature of the Mission's strategy, it will be necessary to monitor a substantial number of custom performance indicators to effectively manage towards and report on the results included in the strategy. As appropriate, the Mission will utilize required FTF indicators for the purposes of managing and reporting on its FTF strategy.

3. Evaluation: Evaluation will be the tool used by the Mission to fill the data gaps that typically – and expectedly – emerge during performance monitoring. Consistent with the new USAID evaluation policy, the Mission will more routinely conduct impact and performance evaluations. Where appropriate, USAID/WA will use the difference-in-difference (counterfactual) approach in analyzing how much of the success can be attributed to its FTF interventions where the opportunity to credibly do so exist. This represents a drastic shift from the current approach of before-after comparisons, which seek to identify whether an outcome related to the objective of the project can be observed and, if it can be observed, the success can be attributable to the intervention. USAID/WA will incorporate strong evaluation functions in the design of FTF interventions and will, from the beginning, gather plausible evidence to reduce the uncertainty about the "difference" a program is making and ensure a system of learning is established.

4. Analysis: An underappreciated component of an effective M&E system is analysis. The West Africa Mission will apply a wide variety of analytic tools, from simple descriptive statistics and the use of frequencies to more complicated time series and comparative analyses (including GIS), to identify trends and patterns that highlight areas of opportunity and/or concern. The Mission will also use modeling to better understand its program's contribution to broader changes and impact.

---

[37] The West Africa Mission will confer with USAID/W and the bilateral USAID missions in the region to avoid "double counting" that might otherwise occur.

ANNEX A. CROSSWALK - ECONOMIC COMMUNITY OF WEST AFRICAN STATES AGRICULTURE POLICY (ECOWAP) INVESTMENT PLAN AND THE U.S. GOVERNMENT FEED THE FUTURE MULTI-YEAR STRATEGY

Core Investment Area	ECOWAP Mobilizing Programs and Actions Supported
1. Increased Use of Climate-Smart Agriculture Practices	Mobilizing Program 2: Promoting a global environment conducive to regional agricultural development • Action 2.2.1.1: Improve knowledge on climate variability and change, and their impacts on agriculture • Action 2.2.1.2: Develop techniques and technologies to adapt to climate change • Action 2.2.1.3: Leverage and transfer techniques and technologies to adapt to climate change • Action 2.3.1.1: Set up a coordinated system of environmental monitoring
2. Increased Regional Availability of Improved Agricultural Inputs for Selected Crops	Mobilizing Program 1: Promote strategic products for food security and food sovereignty • Action 1.1.1.3: Strengthen input distribution networks • Action 1.1.1.5 Develop and disseminate new seeds • Action 1.1.1.7: Develop and help enforce regulation for agricultural inputs (fertilizers, pesticides, seeds) • Action 1.1.1.8: Promote local fertilizer production
3. Increased Regional Trade in Key Agricultural Commodities	Mobilizing Program 1: Promote strategic products for food security and food sovereignty • Action 1.1.3.1: Support regional networks of producer organizations and inter-professional associations • Action 1.1.3.2: Support inter-regional trade of food products • Action 1.1.4.1: Regulate, standardize and certify products and training available to stakeholders • Action 1.2.1.1: Ensure animal health • Action 1.2.3.2: Strengthen the organization of inter-professional associations and structure animal production chains Mobilizing Program 2: Promoting a global environment conducive to regional agricultural development • Action 2.3.3.1: Strengthen production mechanisms and improve dissemination of information on markets and trade opportunities • Action 2.3.2.2: Conduct periodic analysis on the advantages and performance of value chains that may be of regional interest
4. Increased Capacity of Regional Agricultural Sector Actors	Mobilizing Program 2: Promoting a global environment conducive to regional agricultural development • Action 2.3.2.3: Develop a regional early warning system for animal feed and water crises • Action 2.3.2.4: Analyze trends in food and nutritional insecurity • Action 2.4.1.1: Support research and training institutions • Action 2.4.1.2: Support regional socio-professional trade organizations Mobilizing Program 3: Reducing food insecurity and promoting sustainable access to food • Action 3.2.1.2: Consolidate nutritional monitoring systems • Action 3.2.2.2: Strengthen national and regional consultative and coordination mechanisms to address the food situation and formulate responses to crises • Action 3.3.1.1: Support the formulation of national contingency plans for managing food crises • Action 3.3.1.2: Formulate a regional contingency plan • Action 3.2.2.2: Strengthen national and regional consultative and coordination mechanisms to address the food situation and formulate responses to crises

ANNEX B. REFERENCES

Abt Associates. 2010. Through Trade: Prospects for Value Chain Development.

Agboh-Noameshie, R., F. M. Kinkingninhoun-Medagbe, and A. Aliou. 2008. Gendered Impact of NERICA Adoption on Farmers' Production and Income in Central Benin No. 11. Advancing Technical Change in African Agriculture. http://purl.umn.edu/52082

Aker, Jenny C. 2008. Does Digital Divide or Provide? The Impact of Cell Phones on Grain Markets in Niger. University of California, Berkeley.

Barrett Nichols, C. Manfre, and D. Rubin. 2009. Promoting Gender Equitable Opportunities: Why it Matters for Agricultural Value Chains. Washington, D.C. USAID.

Beintema, N. and F. Marcantonio. 2007. Women's Participation in Agricultural Research and Higher Education Trends in Sub-Saharan Africa. ASTI. Washington, DC, IFPRI and Nairobi: Gender and Diversity Program, CGIAR.

Birdsall, N. et al. 1995. Inequality and Growth Revisited: Lessons from East Asia. World Bank Economic Review 9.

Boone, Peter, Charles J.D. Stathacos, and Rose Lum Wanzie. 2008. Maize Value Chain Assessment, ATP Draft Technical Report No. 1, ATP.

Breman, H., B. Fofana and A. Mando. The Lesson of Drente's 'Essen' Soil Nutrient Depletion in Sub-Saharan Africa and Management Strategies for Soil Replenishment. in Braimoh, A.K. and P.L.G. Vlek, Land Use and Soil Resources. Springer Media.

Bromley, Daniel W. 2010. Exports, Employment, and Incomes in West Africa, West Africa Trade Hub.

Bromley, Daniel W. and Jeremy D. Foltz. 2011. "Sustainability Under Siege: Transport Costs and Corruption on West Africa's Trade Corridors," Natural Resources Forum, (forthcoming).

Bumba, B.L., M. Johnson, and P. Fuentes. 2010. Policy Considerations for Improving Regional Fertilizer Markets in West Africa, IFDC and IFPRI.

CILSS. Operational Plan 2011.

CILSS. 2009. Process of Integration of Nutritional Indicators in Food Security Monitoring in the Sahel and West Africa.

CORAF. 2008. Operational Plan 2008 – 2013.

CORAF. Revised Strategic Plan for Agriculture Research and Development Cooperation For West and Central Africa 2007-2016.

Coulibaly, Oumar and Dr. Seydou Sidibé. 2008. Évaluation Sous Régionale de la Chaîne de Valeurs Bétail/Viande, Rapport Technique ATP N° 3. ATP.

Deininger, K. and L. Squire. 1998. New Ways of Looking at Old Issues: Inequality and Growth. Journal of Development Economics 57.

Diao, Xinshin, Shenggen Fan, Derek Headey, Michael Johnson, Alejandro Nin Pratt, and Bingxin Yu. 2008. Accelerating Africa's Food Production in Response to Rising Food Prices – Impacts and Requisite Actions, Washington, D.C. IFPRI ReSAKSS Working Paper No. 3.

Dorosh, Paul, Hyoung-Gun Wang, Liang You, and Emily Schmidt. 2009. Crop Production and Road Connectivity in Sub-Saharan Africa: A Spatial Analysis, Washington, D.C. World Bank, Africa Infrastructure Diagnostic, Working Paper 19.

ECOWAS. 2011. Regional Investment Plan; updated version submitted to the Expert and Ministerial Meeting of the Specialized Technical Committee on Agriculture, Environment and Water Resources, Accra, Ghana.

ECOWAS Commission. 2010. Summary Note on Policy Instruments for the Implementation of ECOWAP/CAADP.

FAO. 2010. Climate-smart Agriculture: Policies, Practices and Financing for Food Security, Adaptation and Mitigation.

Freitas, Sandra. 2010. Gender Differentiated Impacts of Climate Change in the Economic Community of West African States (ECOWAS) Sub-region: Evidence and Implications. Women and Environment Development Organization.

Haggblade, Steven. 2010. Unscrambling Africa: Regional Requirements for Achieving Food Security.

Haussman, R. et al. 2010. The Global Gender Gap Report 2010. Geneva, Switzerland. World Economic Forum. OECD http://genderindex.org.

IFPRI. 2006. Regional Strategic Alternatives for Agriculture-led Growth and Poverty Reduction in West Africa.

International Institute for Environment and Development. 2010. Modern and Mobile: The Future of Livestock Production in Africa's Drylands.

International Resources Group (IRG). 2010. Analyse de la Filière Engrais au Sénégal et de son Evolution sur la Période 2000 – 2009.

Johnson Michael. et al. 2008. Regional Strategic Alternatives for Agriculture-led Growth and Poverty Reduction in West Africa, ReSAKSS Working Paper No. 22

Limao, N., and Venables. 2001. Infrastructure, Geographic Disadvantages, and Transport Costs. World Bank Economic Review 15 (3).

Marenya, P.P. and C.B. Barrett. 2009. State-Conditional Fertilizer Yield Response on Western Kenyan Farms. American Journal of Agricultural Economics.

Masika, Rachel and Susan Joekes. 1997. Environmentally Sustainable Development and Poverty: A gender analysis. Report No.52. Brighton, UK. BRIDGE. http://www.bridge.ids.ac.uk//bridge/reports/re52.pdf.

Ofei, Frank and Daniel Plunkett. 2009. Trade Barriers Assessment for Intra-Regional Trade in Livestock, Maize and Onions/Shallots, ATP.

Orozco, Manuel. 2006. West African Financial Flows and Opportunities for People and Small Businesses. Carana Corporation. Washington, D.C.

Ouisumbing, A. 2003. Household Decisions, Gender and Development: A Synthesis of Recent Research. Washington, D.C., *IFPRI* and the Johns Hopkins University Press.

Poulton, Colin, Geoff Tyler, Peter Hazell, Andrew Dorward, Jonathan Kydd, and Mike Stockbridge. 2008. Commercial Agriculture in Africa: Lessons from Success and Failure, World Bank and FAO.

Rasmussen, N. et al. 2010. Transport and Logistics Costs on the Tema-Ouagadougou Corridor, West Africa Trade Hub Technical Report 25, West Africa Trade Hub.

Rubin, Deborah. 2011. USAID/WA Gender Analysis, Cultural Practices.

Sabates-Wheeler, R. 2004. Asset Inequality and Agricultural Growth: How Are Patterns of Asset Inequality Established and Reproduced. Brighton, UK, IDS.

Schmida, Steve, and Rockfeler Herisse. 2011. Evaluation of West Africa Seeds Alliance (WASA).

Staatz, John M. and Niama Nango Dembélé. 2007. Agriculture for Development in Sub-Saharan Africa, Background paper for WDR 2008, Michigan State University, May 2007.

Teravaninthorn, S and G Raballand. 2008. Transport Prices and Costs in Africa: A Review of the Main International Corridors. Working Paper 14. Africa Infrastructure Sector Diagnostic—World Bank, Washington D.C.

USAID/West Africa Agribusiness and Trade Promotion (ATP) Project. 2009. Annual Progress Report: October 2008-September 2009

US Department of Agriculture. 2010. Capabilities in Agricultural Markets, Capacity Building and Trade.

United Nations Economic Commission for Africa (UNECA), African Union Commission (AUC) and African Development Bank (AfDB). 2010. Gender and Intra African Trade: The Case of West Africa (Chapter 12) in *Assessing Regional Integration in Africa VI: Enhancing Intra African Trade.* Addis Ababa.

West African Seeds Alliance. 2009. Seed Production and Constraints in West Africa: An Assessment of the Seed Systems in Ghana, Nigeria, Mali, Niger, Senegal, Burkina Faso, Togo, and Benin.

West Africa Trade Hub. 2011. Agricultural Trade Policy and Transport in West Africa.

West Africa Trade Hub, 2009. Benin, Burkina, Côte d'Ivoire, Ghana, Niger, Nigeria, Mali, and Togo Gap Analysis: ECOWAS Free Trade Area.

West Africa Trade Hub. 2010. Gap Analysis: ECOWAS Free Trade Area, Preliminary Findings, WA Trade Hub Technical Report #33.

World Bank. 2008. World Development Indicators. Washington, D.C.

Zerelli, S and A Cook, 2010. <u>Trucking to West Africa's Landlocked Countries: Market Structure and Conduct Technical Report No. 32</u>. West Africa Trade Hub